GW01276061

MY FIRST JUNGLE ATLAS

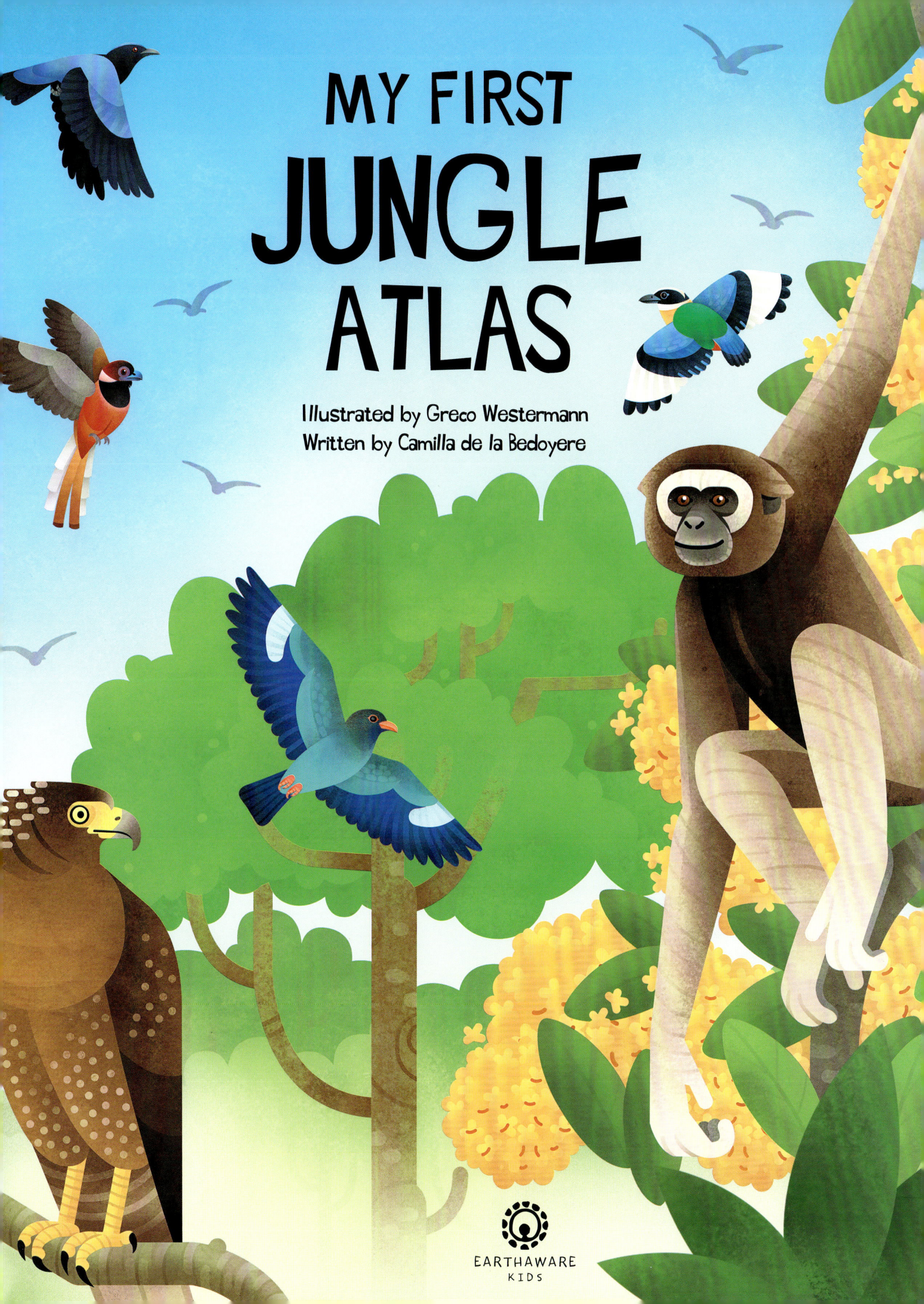

Illustrated by Greco Westermann
Written by Camilla de la Bedoyere

EARTHAWARE
KIDS

Illustrated by Greco Westermann
Written by Camilla de la Bedoyere
Zoology Consultant: Dr Natalie Pilakouta, University of St Andrews

EARTHAWARE KIDS

Copyright © EarthAware Kids, 2025

All rights reserved. No part of this publication may be reproduced, distributed or transmitted in any form or by any means, including photocopying, recording, or other electronic or mechanical methods, without the prior written permission of the publisher, except in the case of brief quotations embodied in critical reviews and certain other noncommercial uses permitted by copyright law.

Published by EarthAware Kids
Created by Weldon Owen Children's Books
An Imprint of Weldon Owen International, L.P.
A subsidiary of Insight International, L.P.
PO Box 3088
San Rafael, CA 94912
www.insighteditions.com

Weldon Owen Childre's Books
Senior Designer: Emma Randall
Senior Editor: Pauline Savage
Editor: Eliza Kirby
Managing Editor: Mary Beth Garhart

Insight Editions
CEO: Raoul Goff
Senior Production Manager: Greg Steffen

ISBN: 979-8-88674-252-7

Manufactured in China by Insight Editions.
First printing, April 2025, DRM0425
10 9 8 7 6 5 4 3 2 1

ROOTS of PEACE   REPLANTED PAPER
Insight Editions, in association with Roots of Peace, will plant two trees for each tree used in the manufacturing of this book.

FSC MIX Paper | Supporting responsible forestry FSC® C188448

CONTENTS

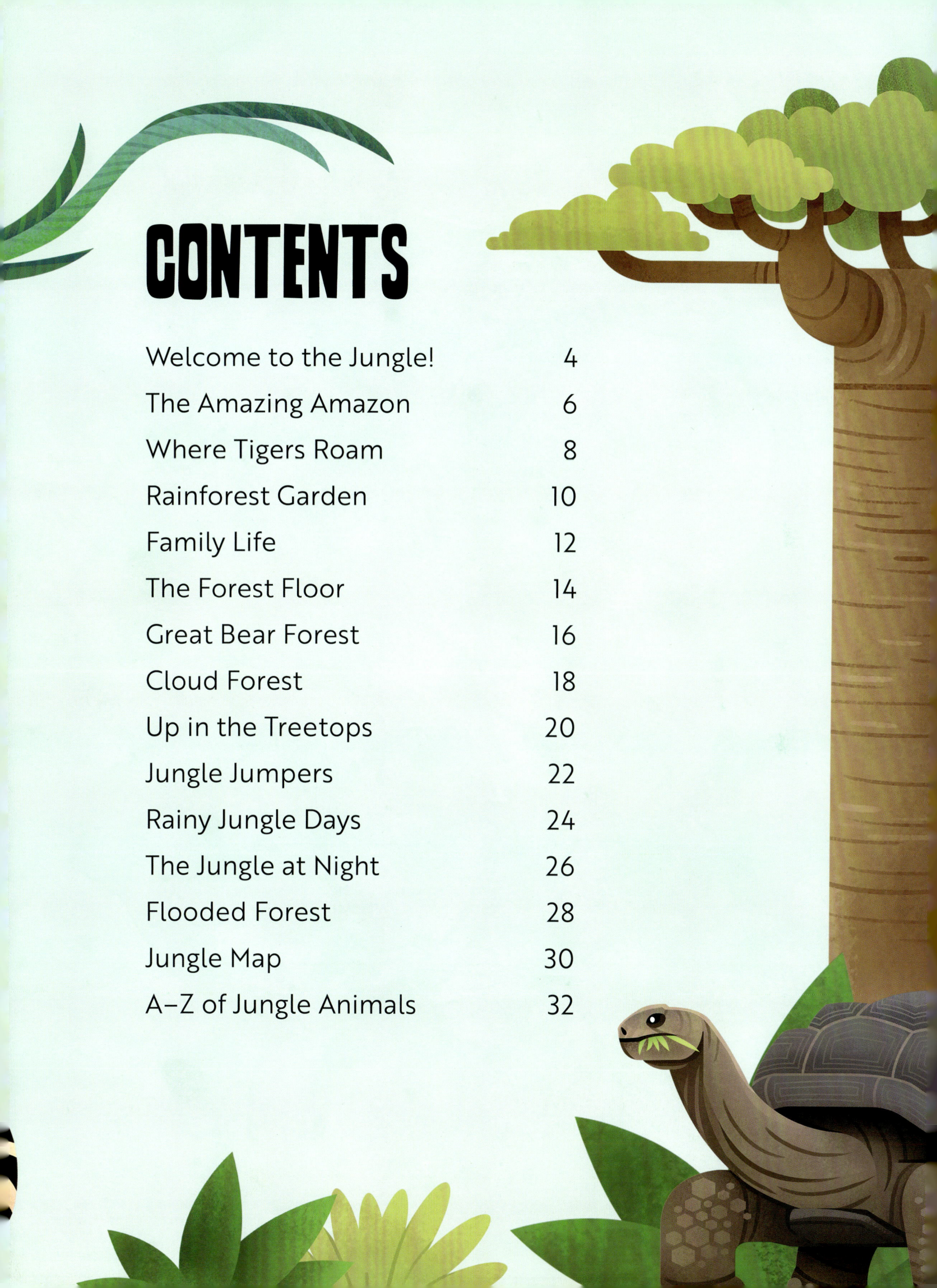

Welcome to the Jungle!	4
The Amazing Amazon	6
Where Tigers Roam	8
Rainforest Garden	10
Family Life	12
The Forest Floor	14
Great Bear Forest	16
Cloud Forest	18
Up in the Treetops	20
Jungle Jumpers	22
Rainy Jungle Days	24
The Jungle at Night	26
Flooded Forest	28
Jungle Map	30
A–Z of Jungle Animals	32

WELCOME TO THE JUNGLE!

In many corners of the world, there are thick forests full of tangled plants. We sometimes call these amazing places jungles. Each is home to thousands of fascinating animals. Some live high up in the tallest trees, while others stay hidden among the branches or on the shadowy forest floor. How many will you spot on your imaginary journey through the most precious habitats on the planet?

Great green macaw

Jaguarundi

Great curassow

Giant anteater

SPOT IT! Find a big bird that is perched high in the treetops.

Black-collared hawk

WAY UP HIGH
The tallest trees grow up to reach the sunlight. This part of the jungle is called the emergent layer. Monkeys and birds often perch up here.

Harpy eagle

Spider monkey

DENSE CANOPY
The canopy is made up of branches and leaves. There is plenty of food in this large and busy habitat. Most jungle animals live here.

Pit viper

Opossum

JUST ABOVE GROUND
Small trees and bushes create the understory layer, where little sunshine reaches. Here, animals that don't fly or climb are more common.

Helmeted iguana

White-lipped peccary

FOREST FLOOR
On the ground, it is damp and shady. There are tree roots, small plants, fungi, and rotting leaves. It teems with insects and other bugs.

Bush dog

Which animal sucks up ants from the forest floor?

5

THE AMAZING AMAZON

In the Amazon rainforest, another hot, steamy day is coming to an end. While many animals settle down for the night, others begin to stir from their sleep. Dusk is the perfect time for them to find food. Predators use the cover of darkness to attack their prey. Other animals scuttle about in the shadows, hoping to hide from those hungry hunters and find themselves a meal.

The Amazon rainforest is the largest tropical jungle in the world. Not only is it home to millions of different animals, but many brightly colored, strange-looking plants grow here, too.

Heliconia

Potoo

BUG CATCHER
The peculiar potoo bird sits perfectly still, pretending to be a branch. It snaps up bugs that fly past.

Margay

WILD CAT HUNTER
The margay can hunt in almost total darkness. It uses its incredible eyesight and great sense of smell to find prey.

SPOT IT! Which animal with green, scaly skin is hiding in a tree?

Squirrel monkey

Emerald tree boa

ON THE MOVE
A squirrel monkey scampers along branches and leaps between trees. She keeps her baby safe from predators.

Bromelid

Silky anteater

DADDY DAYCARE
Baby emperor tamarins are cared for mostly by their fathers. These little monkeys live in large family groups.

Poison dart frog

Emperor tamarin

TREE HUGGER
Silky anteaters use their curly tails and strong, curved claws to cling to branches. They catch ants using their long, sticky tongues.

Hoatzin

STINKY BIRD
Hoatzins are known as stinkbirds because they munch on leaves, which are hard to digest. The birds smell like manure and burp a lot!

Can you find two colorful plants?

7

WHERE TIGERS ROAM

Welcome to the Indian jungle, where there has been no rain for weeks. Everything has turned dry and dusty. People once lived here, but now monkeys dart about the empty, ruined buildings. As the sun sets, mighty tigers are on the prowl. They know this is the best time to hunt because thirsty deer, birds, bears, and monkeys will be gathering to drink at the waterhole.

Flame of the forest tree

MAMA BEAR
Sloth bears often raid bees' nests to get to the yummy honey inside. Mothers carry their cubs on their back to keep them safe.

Gray langur

Sloth bear

FINE FEATHERS
Peacocks strut around the jungle. They raise their long feathers to create a huge fan of shimmering blues and greens.

Indian peacock

Bengal tiger

SPOT IT! Which animal is sleeping in the shade?

Banyan tree

Striped hyena

SNOOZING SCAVENGER
A striped hyena enjoys a nap before mealtime. It will be happy to eat any of the tiger's leftovers.

KING OF THE JUNGLE
Tigers are the silent, stealthy hunters that rule this jungle. They watch and wait for the perfect time to attack their prey.

WATCH OUT!
Sambar deer are always on the lookout for danger. They use their sharp antlers to fight each other—and tigers.

Sambar deer

Can you find a tree with leaves that look like flames?

9

RAINFOREST GARDEN

In the far northeast of Australia is a large and ancient rainforest. It is so old that dinosaurs once plodded along beneath its tall trees and giant ferns. Today, the rainforest is home to plants that are found nowhere else on Earth. Among the many creatures that live here is the huge cassowary. This flightless bird is known as the rainforest gardener. It spreads fruit seeds around in its droppings, helping new plants to grow.

Ulysses butterfly

FLUTTER BY
Large, colorful butterflies, like the spectacular Ulysses butterfly, flutter between the trees and lay their eggs on leaves.

Tree kangaroo

LONG-LEGGED LEAPER
A tree kangaroo is at home up in the trees, leaping between the branches. It carries its young in a pouch on its front.

Flying fox

Striped possum

HUNTING BUGS
Striped possums use their long fingers to dig grubs out of tree bark and pick beetles and caterpillars off leaves.

Cassowary plum tree

Kingfisher

Duck-billed platypus

Forest dragon

PECULIAR PLATYPUS
Duck-billed platypuses are unusual mammals. They are furry but lay eggs like a bird and have a bill-shaped mouth.

Cassowary chick

GARDEN BIRD
The cassowary has a thick layer of fluffy feathers. This helps to protect it from sharp thorns in the undergrowth.

Cassowary

SPOT IT!
Which animals are hanging upside down? Find a long-beaked bird that catches fish.

11

FAMILY LIFE

The hot, wet Congo rainforest in Africa is home to many animals, including gorillas. These gentle apes live in groups called troops. They spend most of the day resting and munching on juicy green leaves and fruit.

Look closely and you will spot other families, too. A stork and her chicks are nesting in the canopy, and some elephants are making their way to the waterhole for a cool drink and a bath.

Gray parrot

Silverback gorilla

BIG AND BRAVE
The large and powerful father of a gorilla family is called a silverback. His job is to protect the other gorillas in his troop.

SUN—LOVING SNAKE
A cobra basks in the sun on a rock. It needs to warm up before taking a dip in the water to hunt for food.

Dwarf crocodile

Congo dwarf water cobra

SPOT IT! What animal is lurking in the waterhole?

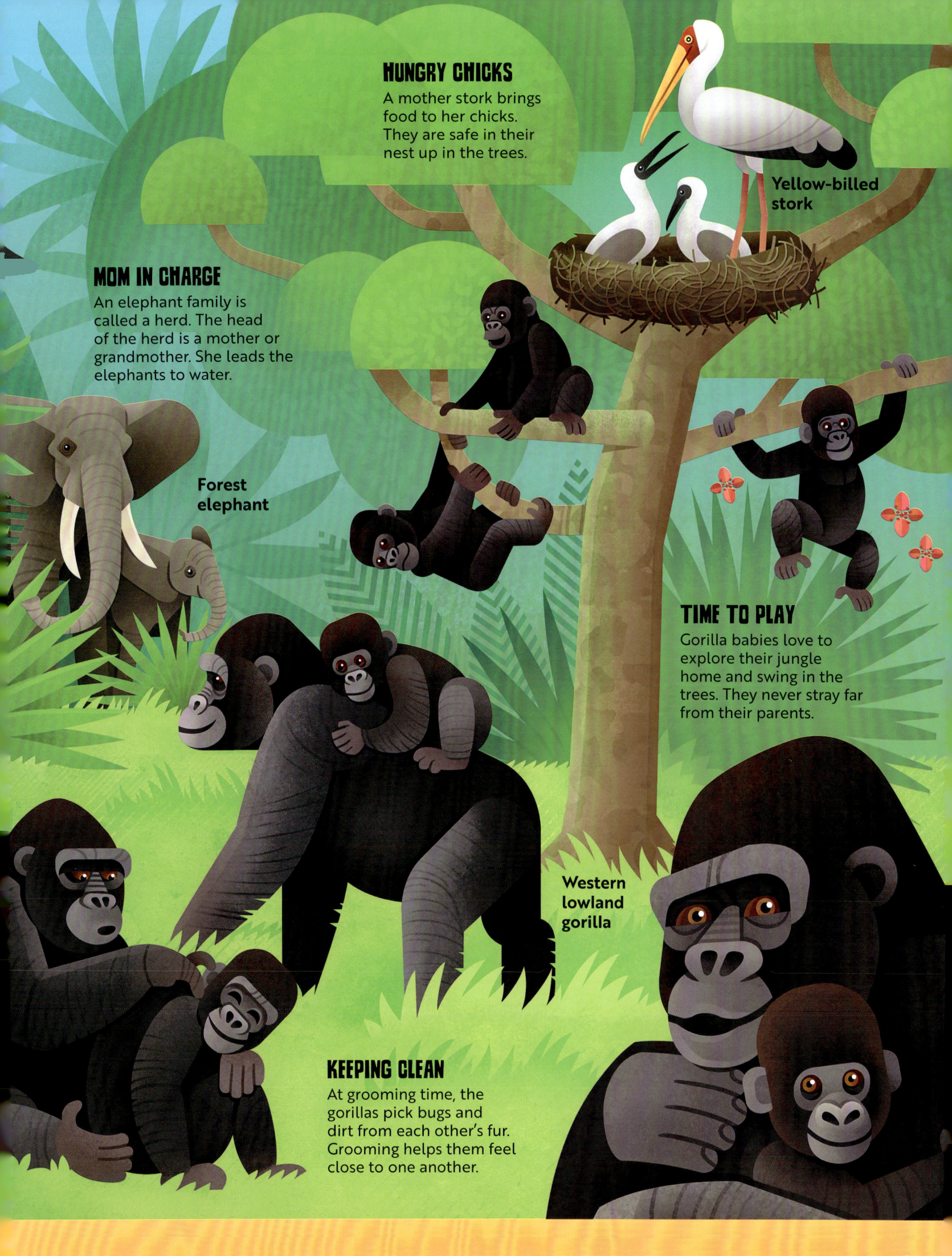

HUNGRY CHICKS
A mother stork brings food to her chicks. They are safe in their nest up in the trees.

Yellow-billed stork

MOM IN CHARGE
An elephant family is called a herd. The head of the herd is a mother or grandmother. She leads the elephants to water.

Forest elephant

TIME TO PLAY
Gorilla babies love to explore their jungle home and swing in the trees. They never stray far from their parents.

Western lowland gorilla

KEEPING CLEAN
At grooming time, the gorillas pick bugs and dirt from each other's fur. Grooming helps them feel close to one another.

How many gorilla babies can you see?

THE FOREST FLOOR

Peer through the dappled shadows of a jungle to discover a hidden world of wildlife. This is the forest floor, where dead leaves fall and colorful fungi grow. Tangled tree roots battle for space and tiny green shoots emerge from seeds, reaching up to the sunlight. Look closely and you will see the forest floor is buzzing with life, from many-legged centipedes to squat frogs and scuttling beetles.

Brazilian wandering spider

Rove beetle

HUNGRY BEETLES
Rove beetles live in the leaf litter and under stones. They eat the insects that they find in animal dung.

STAY AWAY!
Lizards and frogs hunt katydids. Its wings have large false eyes to scare predators away.

Peacock katydid

Amazonian giant centipede

MEGAMOUTH
A Surinam horned frog ambushes small animals that pass by, gulping them down in its huge mouth.

Surinam horned frog

SPOT IT! Find a creature that has eight legs.

MARCHING ANTS
Leafcutter ants use their scissorlike jaws to cut leaves into small pieces. They carry them back to use in their nest.

Leafcutter ant

CLEANUP CREW
Many bugs, such as cockroaches, keep the forest floor clean by eating rotting plants and dead animals.

Cockroach

Green iguana

JUNGLE GIANT
Some jungle centipedes grow longer than your hand! They kill their prey with venomous claws and jaws.

BASKING LIZARD
The forest floor is mostly dark and damp, but a baby green iguana finds a little shaft of sunlight to warm itself up.

How many leafcutter ants can you count?

GREAT BEAR FOREST

On the western coast of North America, a precious rainforest grows. In Canada's Great Bear Forest, cool clouds of mist fill the valleys. Wolves prowl in search of deer to hunt, and trees can live for more than a thousand years. Ghostly white "spirit bears" climb the ancient trees, and salmon leap out of the crystal-clear rivers. The fish make a tasty meal for many of the jungle's animals.

Bald eagle

FISH SNATCHER
Bald eagles use their mighty talons to pluck salmon out of rivers. They also steal fish from other birds of prey!

LOOK AND LISTEN
A Sitka deer must stay alert at all times. There is danger in the shadows, where packs of wolves wait to pounce.

Gray wolf

Sitka deer

SPIRIT BEARS
Some black bears are born with creamy-white fur. They are known as spirit bears. This mother bear has one white cub and one black one!

FLAME BIRD
With bright, flamelike colors, western tanagers are easy to spot in the forest canopy. They snap up insects on leaves and bark.

Western tanager

Grizzly bear

EXPERT FISHER
Grizzly bears feast on salmon that swim upriver. They quickly grab the fish as they leap out of the water.

Salmon

Spirit bear

Cougar

SOLO PREDATOR
Cougars hunt alone. They hide from their prey before making a surprise attack.

Mink

HUNGRY HUNTER
A mink can find plenty of food around a river. It hunts rats, mice, fish, frogs, and birds.

SPOT IT!
How many salmon can you spot? Which predator hunts in a pack?

17

CLOUD FOREST

Blue morpho butterfly

It always feels wet in Costa Rica's Cloud Forest, even when it isn't raining. Up in the mountains of this Central American jungle, the air is cool and damp, and the clouds hang so low you can almost touch them. Plants grow thick and lush, providing plenty of food for the animals that live here. Listen for the slow, steady flapping of a butterfly's wings as it flutters by and the booming call of a howler monkey.

BRILLIANT BIRD
The quetzal is one of the forest's most colorful birds. It has long tail feathers that hang like streamers as it flies.

Quetzal

ALERT AGOUTI
An agouti keeps a lookout for ocelots. If one attacks, it races to its underground den or leaps high up into the air to escape.

Tapir

SNIFF AND SNORT
Tapirs snuffle around on the forest floor, grazing on plants. They snort, stamp, and screech if they sense danger.

Agouti

SPOT IT! Which animal has a spotted coat?

Howler monkey

Blue morpho butterfly

SONIC BOOMER
Furry howler monkeys bellow loudly to warn other monkeys off. Their calls can be heard from far away.

SLOW MOTION
Sloths live in the canopy. They hang upside down in trees and move very, very slowly.

Ocelot

Three-toed sloth

SPOTTED CAT
Small and agile, the ocelot is an expert hunter. It leaps and climbs between the trees and the forest floor.

PRICKLY SKIN
A porcupine defends itself using sharp, needlelike spikes called quills. These grow out of its dark, furry skin.

Mexican hairy dwarf porcupine

Can you find four blue morpho butterflies?

UP IN THE TREETOPS

Jungles can be noisy places, especially up in the canopy. Danum Valley in Borneo is home to some of the world's tallest tropical trees. More animals live in the treetops than anywhere else in the forest. Here beneath the beautiful blue sky, there are bugs buzzing, birds squawking, frogs croaking, and gibbons hooting to each other.

SNAKE CATCHER
Crested serpent eagles perch on the tallest trees. They hunt birds and lizards, and even grab long snakes in their talons.

BLUE BIRD
Dollarbirds flit between trees, using their bright red beaks to snatch flying insects out of the air.

Dollarbird

Diard's trogon

JUNGLE SINGER
Jungle birds, such as the colorful Diard's trogon, sing to each other. This bird's call is a gentle "caw-caw-caw."

Wallace's flying frog

Crested serpent eagle

SPOT IT! Can you name the five different types of bird?

CLEVER BIRD
Blue-winged pitta birds eat insects. They also eat snails because they have learned how to bash them against stones to crack the snail shells open.

FOREST FAIRIES
There is plenty of food in the canopy, such as leaves, seeds, berries, and fruits. Asian fairy bluebirds mostly eat fruit.

Blue-winged pitta

Asian fairy bluebird

Gibbon

JUNGLE SWINGER
Unlike monkeys, gibbons don't have tails. They leap between trees and use their long arms to swing between branches.

FLYING FROG
A Wallace's flying frog can glide like a parachute between trees. It spreads out its long legs and webbed feet—and leaps!

Which animal uses its feet to "fly"?

21

JUNGLE JUMPERS

The magical island of Madagascar split from the rest of Africa almost ninety million years ago. Many of the animals and plants, including bouncy lemurs and mysterious fossas, are rare and precious. They are found nowhere else.

The jungles of Madagascar are mostly lush and rainy or dry with many thorny trees. Giant baobab trees are known as the "mothers of the forest" because they are the oldest living things here. Some are more than a thousand years old.

Coquerel's sifaka

LEAPING LEMUR
Coquerel's sifakas are a type of lemur. They use their long legs to leap up to 30 feet through the air. They also hop across the ground like a kangaroo.

Common brown lemur

COLORFUL REPTILE
Chameleons can change the color of their scaly skins. They shoot out a long, sticky tongue to grab bugs.

Fossa

SHY HUNTER
A fossa looks like a cat, and it hunts like one, too. It silently waits for prey to pass by before pouncing.

Baobab tree

GENTLE GIANT
Wild Aldabra giant tortoises are very rare. They graze on low-growing plants and can live for more than a hundred years.

Panther chameleon

Crested coua

Aldabra giant tortoise

SPOT IT!
How many baobab trees can you count? Which animals have long tails?

23

RAINY JUNGLE DAYS

All morning, strong sunshine heats up this steamy rainforest on the island of Sumatra. By the afternoon, gray clouds have gathered above the canopy, and heavy rain begins to pour down. Some animals use this time to take a bath. Others shelter and wait for the rain to pass. This daily mix of sun and rain is perfect for jungle plants. Look for two of the stinkiest types: the tall titan arum and the giant rafflesia flower. They smell like rotting meat!

Rhinoceros hornbill

Sumatran elephant

HIDEY-HOLES
Male hornbills bring food to their mates, who hide in tree holes to keep their eggs and chicks safe from predators.

Rafflesia

TAKING A SHOWER
The Sumatran elephant's trunk is useful for many things. It can tear leaves from the trees or become a shower hose!

STRIPY PIG
A family of wild boar is looking for food. The piglets have stripy fur, which helps them hide in the dappled forest.

SPOT IT! Which animal has made an umbrella from jungle leaves?

Orangutan

Durian fruit

Common gliding lizard

ORANGE APES
Orangutans spend most of their lives in trees, eating fruit and sleeping. Their favorite food is the smelly, yellow durian fruit.

LEAPING LIZARD
Gliding lizards have flaps of skin between their legs. They leap from branches and glide to the ground or between trees.

MUD BATH
The Sumatran rhinoceros loves to wallow in mud. These animals are rare and shy, so few people have ever seen one.

Titan arum

Wild boar

Wild boar piglet

Sumatran rhinoceros

How many durian fruit are hanging from the tree?

THE JUNGLE AT NIGHT

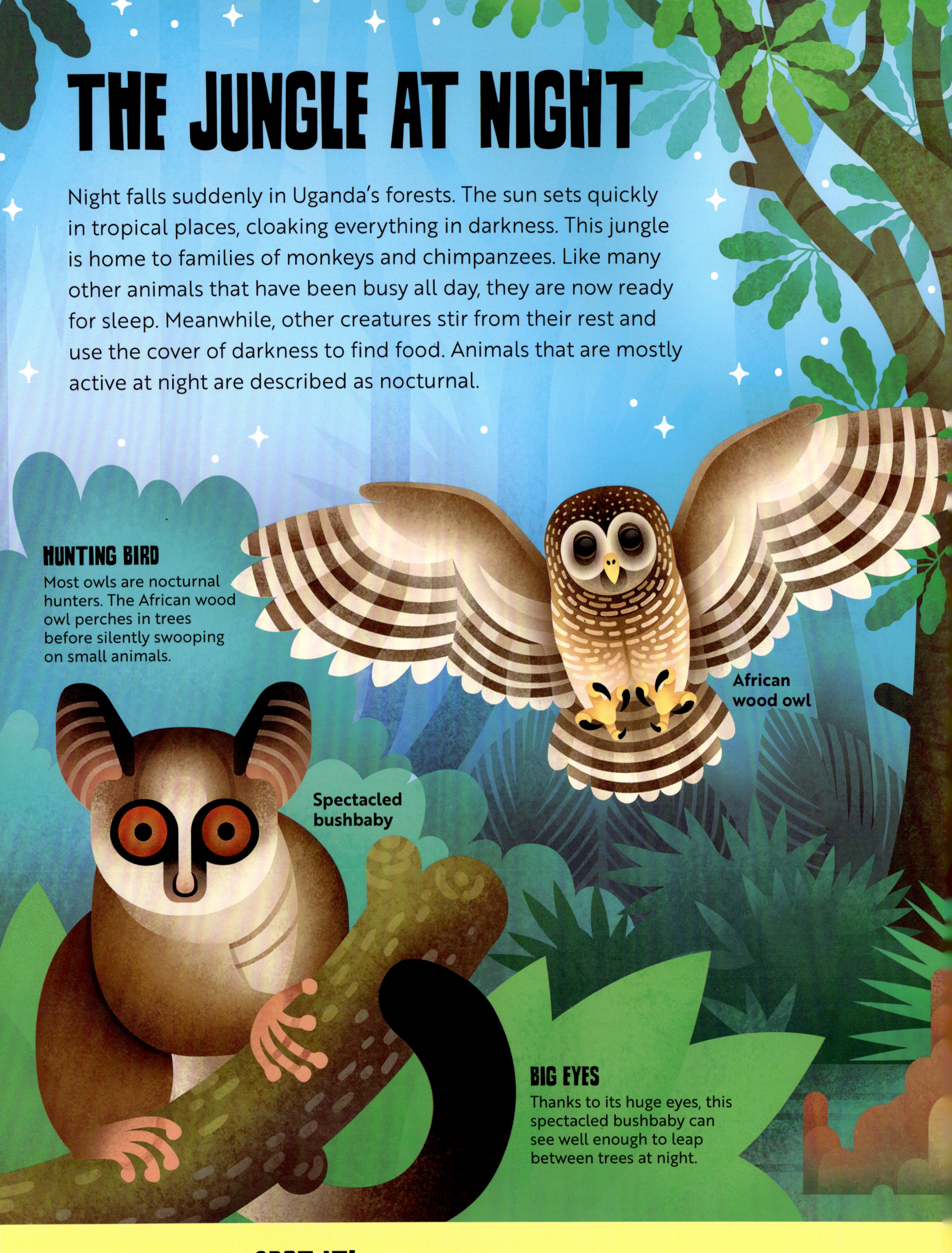

Night falls suddenly in Uganda's forests. The sun sets quickly in tropical places, cloaking everything in darkness. This jungle is home to families of monkeys and chimpanzees. Like many other animals that have been busy all day, they are now ready for sleep. Meanwhile, other creatures stir from their rest and use the cover of darkness to find food. Animals that are mostly active at night are described as nocturnal.

HUNTING BIRD
Most owls are nocturnal hunters. The African wood owl perches in trees before silently swooping on small animals.

Spectacled bushbaby

African wood owl

BIG EYES
Thanks to its huge eyes, this spectacled bushbaby can see well enough to leap between trees at night.

SPOT IT! Which animal is carrying a baby?

Chimpanzee

Noack's roundleaf bat

TIME FOR BED
Chimps build a new nest in trees each night. They weave branches and leaves together to make a soft, cozy bed.

FOUND WITH SOUND
A Noack's roundleaf bat uses sounds and echoes to find prey, such as flying insects. This is called echolocation.

Emperor moth

Leopard

NIGHT SIGHT
Leopards prowl at night, using their superb eyesight to spot any signs of movement in the undergrowth.

STICKY TONGUE
Ground pangolins use their sense of smell to find food in the dark. They catch ants with their long, sticky tongue.

Ground pangolin

How many flying animals can you see?

27

FLOODED FOREST

The Amazon River is the world's largest river. It brings water and life to the rainforests of South America. When heavy rains pour, the river swells until it bursts its banks and floods the forests. Now there are swampy wetlands where many animals can find food. While some animals live in the river all the time, others are visitors that will return to dry land once they have feasted.

Agami heron

HUGE RODENTS
Capybara love to wallow in the shallows. They are good swimmers and can hold their breath underwater for five minutes.

Capybara

Yellow-spotted river turtle

SUN SEEKER
River turtles like to be warm. They find logs or stones to sit on and bask in the sunshine for hours at a time.

Boto

GIANT SNAKE
A huge anaconda hides underwater, waiting to ambush its prey. This is one of the world's biggest snakes.

BEAUTIFUL BOTO
The boto, or pink river dolphin, hunts for fish in the slow-flowing, murky water of the Amazon River.

Green anaconda

SPOT IT! Which two animals like to hunt caimans?

Uakari monkey

I SPY
Giant otters are fast and powerful predators. They stare at the water, searching for fish—and small caimans—to eat.

Giant otter

SWIMMING CAT
Jaguars usually live near rivers. They attack deer, turtles, snakes, capybaras, and even fierce caimans.

Jaguar

Baby caiman

BIG TEETH
Piranha fish hunt in packs. Their scissorlike teeth are perfect for slicing through fish skin and small bones.

Red-bellied piranha

GIANT FISH
The massive arapaima can grow to 10 feet. It needs to come to the surface every 10–20 minutes to breathe.

Arapaima

Which animal is wallowing with its baby?

29

GREAT BEAR FOREST

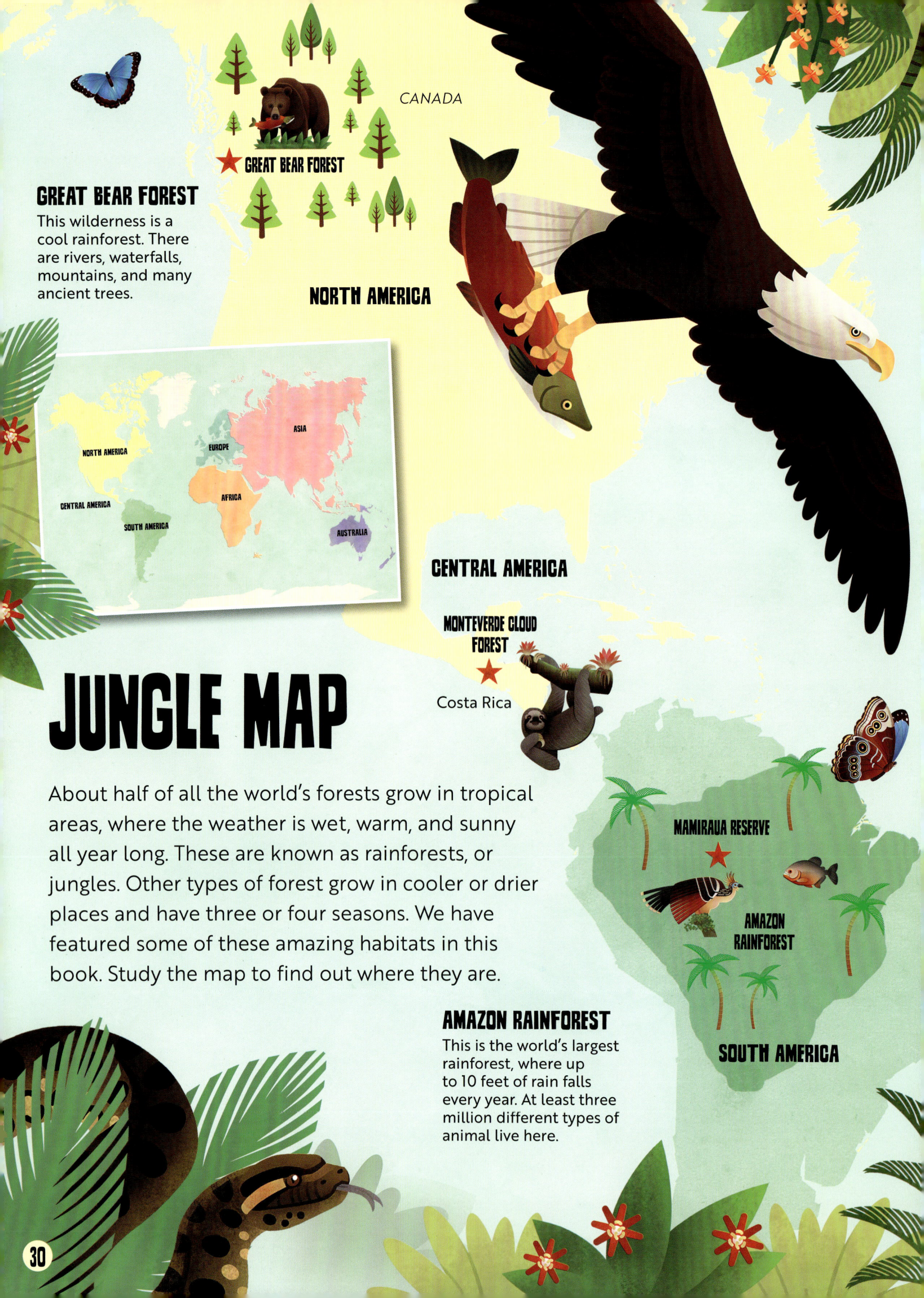

This wilderness is a cool rainforest. There are rivers, waterfalls, mountains, and many ancient trees.

CANADA

GREAT BEAR FOREST

NORTH AMERICA

NORTH AMERICA
EUROPE
ASIA
CENTRAL AMERICA
AFRICA
SOUTH AMERICA
AUSTRALIA

CENTRAL AMERICA

MONTEVERDE CLOUD FOREST

Costa Rica

JUNGLE MAP

About half of all the world's forests grow in tropical areas, where the weather is wet, warm, and sunny all year long. These are known as rainforests, or jungles. Other types of forest grow in cooler or drier places and have three or four seasons. We have featured some of these amazing habitats in this book. Study the map to find out where they are.

MAMIRAUA RESERVE

AMAZON RAINFOREST

AMAZON RAINFOREST

This is the world's largest rainforest, where up to 10 feet of rain falls every year. At least three million different types of animal live here.

SOUTH AMERICA

ASIA

RANTHAMBORE NATIONAL PARK

INDIA

INDIAN FOREST
This tiger reserve in northern India contains tropical dry forests where the trees shed their leaves in dry weather.

DANUM VALLEY RESERVE

GUNUNG LEUSER NATIONAL PARK

BORNEO

SUMATRA

AFRICA

INDONESIAN ISLANDS
The islands of Sumatra and Borneo have many tropical rainforests. The Gunung Leuser forest grows over mountains and is home to orangutans and elephants.

UGANDA

CONGO RAINFOREST

KIBALE NATIONAL PARK

CONGO RAINFOREST
This forest in Africa is mostly warm and wet, with some areas having dry seasons. Gorillas and pangolins are found here.

MADAGASCAR

AUSTRALIA RAINFOREST
Daintree is the largest tropical forest in Australia and the oldest in the world. More than nine hundred different types of tree grow here.

DAINTREE NATIONAL PARK

AUSTRALIA

A–Z OF JUNGLE ANIMALS

African wood owl, 26
Agami heron, 28
Agouti, 18
Aldabra giant tortoise, 23
Amazonian giant centipede, 14-15
Arapaima, 29
Asian fairy bluebird, 21

Bald eagle, 16
Bengal tiger, 8–9
Black-collared hawk, 5
Blue morpho butterfly, 18–19
Blue-winged pitta, 21
Boto, 28
Brazilian wandering spider, 14
Bush dog, 5

Caiman, 29
Capybara, 28
Cassowary, 11
Chimpanzee, 27
Cockroach, 15
Common brown lemur, 22
Common gliding lizard, 25
Congo dwarf water cobra, 12
Coquerel's sifaka, 22–23
Cougar, 17
Crested coua, 22–23
Crested serpent eagle, 20

Diard's trogon, 20
Dollarbird, 20
Duck-billed platypus, 11
Dwarf crocodile, 12

Emerald tree boa, 7
Emperor moth, 27
Emperor tamarin, 7

Flying fox, 10
Forest dragon, 11
Forest elephant, 13
Fossa, 23

Giant anteater, 4
Giant otter, 29
Gibbon, 21
Great curassow, 4
Great green macaw, 4
Green anaconda, 28
Green iguana, 15
Gray langur, 8
Gray parrot, 12
Gray wolf, 16
Grizzly bear, 17
Ground pangolin, 27

Harpy eagle, 5
Helmeted iguana, 5
Hoatzin, 7
Howler monkey, 19

Indian peacock, 8

Jaguar, 29
Jaguarundi, 4

Kingfisher, 11

Leafcutter ant, 15
Leopard, 27

Margay, 6
Mexican hairy dwarf porcupine, 19
Mink, 17

Noack's roundleaf bat, 27

Ocelot, 19
Opossum, 5
Orangutan, 25

Panther chameleon, 23
Peacock katydid, 14
Pit viper, 5
Poison dart frog, 7
Potoo, 6

Quetzal, 18

Red-bellied piranha, 29
Rhinoceros hornbill, 24
Rove beetle, 14

Salmon, 16–17
Sambar deer, 9
Silky anteater, 7
Silverback gorilla, 12
Sitka deer, 16
Sloth bear, 8
Spectacled bushbaby, 26
Spider monkey, 5
Spirit bear, 16–17
Squirrel monkey, 7
Striped hyena, 9
Striped possum, 10
Sumatran elephant, 24
Sumatran rhinoceros, 25
Surinam horned frog, 14

Tapir, 18
Three-toed sloth, 19
Tree kangaroo, 10

Uakari monkey, 29
Ulysses butterfly, 10

Wallace's flying frog, 20
Western lowland gorilla, 12–13
Western tanager, 16
White-lipped peccary, 5
Wild boar, 24–25

Yellow-billed stork, 13
Yellow-spotted river turtle, 28

32